Archway Publishing books may be ordered through booksellers or by contacting:

Archway Publishing
1663 Liberty Drive
Bloomington, IN 47403
www.archwaypublishing.com
844-669-3957

Editor - Michael John Bishop

ISBN: 978-1-6657-0767-1 (sc)
ISBN: 978-1-6657-0768-8 (hc)
ISBN: 978-1-6657-0769-5 (e)

Print information available on the last page.

Archway Publishing rev. date: 07/28/2021

Dedicated to all the Shine Kids! You're Talented, Gifted and Blessed Go Follow Your Dreams!

Do what you love to do!

Do what you love to do and always be true!
Do what makes you happy and puts a smile on you,
because you only live once and there is no time to waiste,
so focus on what you enjoy and your dreams you should chase!

You only get one life so make the best
and do what you love and forget all the rest!
The most important thing is that you enjoy what you do,
so joy and happiness are bestowed amongst you!
Too many people live for others!
They want approval and acceptance until they discover
that the one they need please is themselves,
and what other people think doesn't matter because only their feelings are felt,
so do what feels good inside
and your journey will be an enjoyable ride!

Refrain

There is no nobility in forcing yourself to do what you don't like!
If it makes you feel empty inside you should surrender the fight,
and do what feels easy like a round peg in a round hole,
and if the shoe fits wear it and burn out the souls,
and have fun at what you love to do
because time is not waisted if it brings joy to you
so forget about the money and the fame,
and whatever you do make sure it's for the love of the game!

Refrain

When you do what you love, it is easy and there is no fight!
It excites your soul and you begin to love life,
and if you do what you enjoy to do,
your passion will lead to progress and success will ensue,
so have the courage to do what you love,
and trust in the Good Lord above
because He wants you to be happy so follow His lead
and do what you love, and in the end you will succeed!

Don't give up!

Don't give up no matter how hard the road gets,
just reach down inside and don't you fret
because if you depend on God He will give you the courage and the strength
to continue on and to go the full length!

Dreams take courage and they are hard to chase,
but if you stay strong and keep the faith,
God will help you all along the way
by giving you what you need day after day,
and if you believe you can achieve you will succeed
by staying positive as you face adversity!
The most important thing is that you don't submit
because it is always too early to give up and quit!

Refrain

When following your dreams there will be clouds of doubt
when you feel hopeless and time is running out,
but there is a silver tint that keeps hope alive,
that the sun will come out and again it will shine,
and that's why you must stick with the fight,
and keep the light lit especially in the night
because when you get in a tight place and everything goes against you!
never give up then because that is when the tide will turn for you!

Refrain

Winners come in all shapes and sizes,
but the one thing they have in common is a big heart that never compromises!
They keep on going and give it their best
as they are faced with trials and character tests
and though they may rest they do not quit
because regret is a pain that is hard to live with!
So, when times get hard and your spirits are down,
pray to God for the courage and the strength until it is found,
and remember this too shall pass,
struggles are hard but they do not last,
and if you dig deep and stick it out,
in the end you will be happy you had decided not to bail out!
So, don't give up because you have it in you
to follow your dreams and have them all come true!

Go for it!

Go for it and give it all you got,
and don't stop until you reach the top!
Keep following your dreams until they come true
and happiness will come to you!

You live once so follow your dreams!
Do what makes you happy and join the winning team!
It might not be easy and there might be trials,
but in the end, it is all worth it if it makes you smile
because life is short, and this is your chance
to shine and give the universe a glance
of what you are which is a shooting star,
and if you do the right things you will go far!

Refrain

Dreams take a lot of work!
You must be dedicated if you want the perks!
Nothing good comes easy, but if you are true to the best that you are,
you will not have to worry about emotional scars!
You will have peace knowing that you gave it your best
and your mind will be at rest
because you gave all that's in you,
so do what it is you know that you gotta to do!

Refrain

God has given you talents and He wants you to use them,
and make the most out of all of them not waiste or abuse them!
He wants you to develop your skills, so in the end you feel
good about yourself and so you don't rob and steal,
or cheat yourself out of your best.
So, be true to yourself and your own conscience!
So shine kids and go follow your dreams
and go for it because you born to gleam!

HAVE FUN!

HAVE FUN and enjoy what you do!
Do what makes you happy and puts a smile on you
because there is a time for work and a time for play,
and one without the other only leads to dismay!

Its' one thing to be serious about your craft
but another thing when you refrain from laughs!
What you are called to do should make you smile,
so good memories will last more than a while!
God wants you to work hard but enjoy life too
and share the good times with family and friends that support you!
So, don't hesitate to have a good time
because to rob yourself of joy is the biggest crime!

Refrain

It's easy to worry and get caught in your head
and stress about everything until you start to dread
but that is not God wants from your life,
He wants you to enjoy yourself so don't resist and fight!
Learn to let go and enjoy your day,
relax and take it easy and learn how to play
because nothing is better for the soul then pure and simple fun,
so when you feel yourself getting tight say Thy will be done!

Refrain

Life is short and time fades away,
so make sure you enjoy all of your days!
Count all the blessing that you have
and you will notice inside you feel happy and glad,
and though there are serious things in life
when the time is right, learn to keep it light
and HAVE FUN in whatever you do,
so when you look back you will grateful for the memories that live inside you!

Do your best!

Do your best, put the effort in,
let God do the rest and you're sure to win
because if you have made the best of what you have,
in the end with yourself you will be glad!

Everyone is different and everyone has their own gifts!
Everyone has unique talents to excel with,
but the one thing always you can do
is give the best that is inside of you!
God made you special and wants you to shine like a star,
and wants you to succeed and go real far,
and He is willing to help you in whatever dreams you are called to pursue,
the only thing He asks is that you give the best that is inside of you!

Refrain

When you do your best, you feel good inside,
and you can walk tall and be filled with pride,
and you can look in the mirror and be happy with what you see
when you do your best consistently!
Once in a while is just not enough;
Every day it should be your aim, even though it can be tough,
but if you pray to God He will come and help you
pull out the best that is inside out you!

Refrain

You must be true to yourself when you ask
the person in the glass if that test you have passed!
Can you look that person straight in the eye
and make no excuses or alibies
because at the end of the day it is between God and you
and you can't fool either one so always be true,
and if you have tried your best then you are a success
no matter how you compare to all the rest
because life doesn't require that we be the best
only that we try our best and nothing less,
so give yourself credit and a pat on the back
for living up to your potential and not holding back
because anything less than the best is to sacrifice the gift,
so do your best and give your spirits a lift!

You can!

You can do what you want to do!
Don't ever let anyone discourage you
because you can succeed if you believe,
so take a chance on yourself and plant a seed!

You are a capable; God has given you gifts
to contribute to the world and give your spirits a lift!
You have something to offer and are able to achieve,
so have faith in yourself and choose to believe,
and never let anyone bring you down,
and stay away from the little minds that carry disparaging sounds,
and hang around with those that believe you can succeed,
and encourage you to believe and achieve
and fulfill your destiny by answering the call God has for you,
so you can make the world a better place by the work that you do!

Refrain

A great attitude always precedes a great performance,
so don't let your spirit become dormant,
and your mind can only hold one thought at a time,
so make it a constructive one so that you begin to shine,
and let positivity control your mood,
and when you fail, always be gentle on yourself and soothe
because it is only education and it will only lead to you getting better,
and if you keep on moving forward during the stormy weather,
eventually the sun will come out and like a flower you will blossom and grow,
and you will be astounded by the progress even though it might have been slow
and you will have the confidence and be happy with what you see,
when you have an attitude of positivity!

Refrain

So, dream big because there is little power in little plans,
and you can achieve anything that God demands!
It might be hard but if you trust in Him,
and have the attitude that I am born to win,
good things will happen when your attitude is right,
so stay on the straight and narrow and your spirit will take flight,
and you will succeed when you say
you can when you look in the mirror each and every day!

Believe + Achieve!

Believe and achieve, strive and drive!
Do the best with what you have and watch yourself climb!
Believe in yourself and you will see
yourself live up to your potential and what you were meant to be!

Hard work, desire and perspiration,
dedication to your craft, hopping hurdles that your facing!
true chasing of your goals and your dreams,
having the courage to go the distance, succeeding by any means,
risk taking, going all out, never jaking,
100 percent given every time, never taking
anything for granted or wasting opportunities,
giving it your best, every day is new to see
progress in yourself when you shoot top shelf,
so give it all you got and when in need ask for help!

Refrain

Pushing yourself when you're tired and run down,
with your game face on, no clowning around
because you play like; you practice so practice the way you want to play,
true champions do it in and out every day,
and give it their best and never settle for less!
So, whether they win or lose, they walk away with pride in their chest,
and stay blessed because of the work put in,
because those who are slothful truly live in sin,
robbing the world of their precious gifts
that God has given them; many are on the list,
so which one do you want to be: the one that hits or misses
the winner or your own worst nemesis!

Refrain

So, the moral of the story is not to sell yourself short,
and don't fall in any traps and get yourself caught!
Keep an open mind and you will find
when you believe in yourself you can accomplish things way beyond what you eyed!
So, dream wide and always do your best,
so that the person in the mirror you don't second-guess!

About the Author

Ryan Lee Nevins is a former professional baseball player, Golden Gloves boxer, New York City marathoner and ultra-marathoner, peer counselor, porter, and award-winning poet. Hailing from New York City, he seeks to help kids through his experiences using poetry and art and through his volunteer work with organizations such as the St. Kevin Care and Share program and the Special Olympics. Visit him online at shinekidsfoundation.com.

*"I can do all things through Christ
who strengthens me."
Phillipians 4:13*

Thy

will

be

done!

Printed in the United States
by Baker & Taylor Publisher Services